Praise for *Frangible Operas*

"In *Frangible Operas*, a couple waits for the bus, 'The old man was turned / toward her in a half-twist, / like a landlocked diver— / ...the only fine fish / in his sea—or, as if she was / the last magic flower...' While the poet teaches poems to prisoners, and listens to the trees and birds, she lets death be everywhere, ever present as rain, hummingbirds, cold air, and clouds. 'We will think we are still dreaming / when the ghosts of the mothers and fathers arrive, / when they hold hands with us, singing.'"

— Joyce Jenkins, editor and publisher of *Poetry Flash*

"Susan Kelly-DeWitt is a seer at the height of her formidable artistic powers, gathering parallel realities, fractured light, music of blue flowers, syllables of leaves, stars fallen in nets we cast, and the unseen seeds of our imaginations, such that with every vulnerable song we experience the wholeness of what's sacred — grief, joy, love, hope in wonder. These exquisite poems, their stunning imagery, expansive and focused, witness 'the wilderness inside us,' even as they "pulse with the energy of the soul's primal blast.'"

— William O'Daly, author of *The New Gods* and translator
   of Pablo Neruda's *Book of Twilight*

Frangible Operas

Poems

Susan Kelly-DeWitt

Gunpowder Press • Santa Barbara
2024

Published by Gunpowder Press
David Starkey, Editor
PO Box 60035
Santa Barbara, CA 93160-0035

Front cover image: Photo by Annie Spratt

ISBN-13: 978-1-957062-15-0

www.gunpowderpress.com

... everything always a trace toward understanding.

— Dean Rader, "Meditation on Comprehension"

Hold hands, hold hands
That when the birds start, none of us is missing.

— Charles Wright, "Self-Portrait"

Contents

III.

IV.

I.

Frangible Operas

Tonight the bells of the flowers ring out, five peals for five petals, the dusky throats of the mystery of blue flowers, crying out to be heard as you pass them where they glow in the center of a polished oak table. And if the table is a Feng Shui bagua for mapping one round section of this particular earth, these flowers are nothing less than the center of their own blue universe—breathing in even the deep blues inside you now, exhaling wholeness with their pollens and shadows; so loudly you stop, forget where you were going—toward a kitchen cupboard, a clear glass tumbler, the muted sounds of the tap—hear only the flowers' blue chimes, their plangent xylophones, frangible operas.

Magnificat

I wish I could carry a tune
for then I would write a simple song
about these blackbirds filling up a pearl
gray sky at dusk, along some river-edge
of winter, peppering the leafless
branches of an ash—

but since I was always instructed
I'd never be able to mouth or croon
a single melody, or hold any key
(except for the type with metal teeth,
to snug-fit the locked) I will have to hum
a poem's whole notes with my pen,
peck the syllables out of fog
and silence, nest them here

where a few words land like ink-
black birds along the notebook's blue
tributaries, its dry white estuaries.

Once I might have penciled them in
—*are they grackles? or Brewer's?*—
as Angels of Death, arriving to herald
some spiritual twilight, missing entirely
the way they're calligraphied like *yuefu*
on a shifting scroll;

how they're gathered together like
choir, or chorale—like busy notes in a Vivaldi
Gloria, a *Magnificat* by Bach; feather and beak

in a living tangle, yes—black bells, onyx
beads strung orderly and wild among so many
invisible rosaries of atoms, molecules, cells—

knitted close while darkness swells,
and a few late blossoms, though trampled
down, glisten on the sweet wet
planet beneath them.

Last Supper

Nothing especially Christian about it
unless you count guilt
which occupied all
the usual empty chairs.

Even the burritos were iconoclastic:
whole wheat tortillas with sunflower
seeds, warmed in the microwave.

Stone-faced Buddha looked on
from his seat by the fireplace.

The still, small voice
whispered: *This is different...*
but I ignored it.

"Eat," she said, and on faith
we passed the old silences
between us, body
and blood.

Songs for the End of Spiritual Winter

Astonishment
that I am here at all.

—=—

What is this magnetic pulsing
I feel under my feet, the earth
veining up, the yellow leaves
of willow, the smoke of burned
fields calling, calling, calling?

What is this vibrating wave
of affection flying down
from each overhanging branch,
the bare and the fruit-laden?

Why does some voice inside
the larkspur or the least frost-
bitten leaf pour into me like
sacred oil?

—=—

This morning a white frost, iced
over grasses, a world of white—
white narcissus in bloom, a few
cold-shattered azaleas, snow white.

Down the street, a red room still
in lamplight, a vase of white roses

shines through the window.
I am outside in the cold and the weak
dawn light, but where am I going—
walking these familiar loops through
the neighborhood, thinking of frost,
thinking of snow and ice.

—=—

Today I am locking pain outside
to fatten like a starved ghost on the meal
of crushed camellia petals, ruined azaleas
and the bewilderment of the dazed

baby waxwing fallen from its nest (fresh
butter trim on its scalloped tailfeathers)
that wandered the street's paved divide
as cars swerved aside, for a while.

—=—

Underneath the bloodworks,
the jittery fleshleaves,
the spider of worry
is awake.

Her spinnerets spin sticky silks;
her small brown jaws work over
the same old hapless moth
of thought.

—=—

October again. I calculate
my life. Nineteen thousand
seven hundred and twenty-two

days. How many
are left? The maple outside
my window loses

its bright lottery
of leaves.

—=—

The books on my shelf, the clever and the plain-
spoken, lean against each other, perfectly at ease.
The electric clock seems comfortable enough
with its own reliable ticking.

—=—

Today I am reacquainting myself with the language
of living things. These leaves I touch are toothed
syllables, serrate flames kindling from green tongues
at the edge of silence. My soul enters the good dirt
—testing the cycles again, the way the dead must
learn to speak a new vernacular.

Korea, 1952

Guilt replays
a newsreel's flickering
trumpet of light:

A scrawny girl
so hungry, so hungry

she rifles trash, eats
broken glass—a morsel
of pain
to fill her belly.

Afternoons at Sacred
Heart Academy, we
say a rosary for the starving

children. Sister
Philomena prays with us,
her onyx rosary
beads anchored
to her thick waist.

Oh those glittering black
buds of salvation...

Parallel Worlds

The surface of the river hooks
light into taut loops

like a crocheted afghan
some winter mother needles
into glitter-lace,

flung against the bare gold
of the levee.

The stars fell to earth
and caught in the nets...

we tossed on the waters
she read to me once
when I was five.

—=—

The skein of dusk
unwinds in a swirl of dry
bindweed; it tangles

in the heart-
shaped leaves of cottonwoods,
in willow skins, in

pickerel weed. Night
falls faster and faster
on the littered shore

where we stand
talking in hoarse
whispers, Mother.

Late Alzheimer's

the beloved poet's wife steered
            him by one elbow through the assembled
crowd the gallery of admiring
            faces beating like moths
against the light flickering out inside
            the dead glass of his eyes

all the incisive elegant words
            all the minutes shrunk to blind
corridors leading to a deserted museum
            the paintings sculptures
vanished some stolen some sorted

            and stored in the museum's basement
the boy with the terrier
            the woman with green eyes
the man with the black apron
            polished shoes with their laces untied

cut glass vases of roses violets lilies
            heavy plates stacked with ripe fruits
cantaloupes plums cherries
            the caterpillar crawling on a freshly cut stem
the butterfly hugging a lettuce leaf

            windblown cypresses on a cliff
            an icy footpath through the snow
            choppy seas fractured light
            even those two bronze lovers
            so knotted so tied

to each other in that kiss that gleam
of muscles veins the centaurs'
loins even the marble
heads of the scholars
all of them were gone yes
only erasure whistled
breathless

        through those halls out of tune toothless
harmonica of the brain's lung

Cold Call

The shifty skeletons of the dead
are trying to sell us something:
the weight of the sky
on our chests...

Their wristwatches never stop,
their cars have infinite warranties,
their Hoovers suck up stars
and loneliness.

Have you ever heard the door-to door
tongues of the dead
                              la-la-la-ing

from under the clean-swept
carpets of grass?

Tonight, all along Riverside Boulevard,
as the traffic whips past
the old cemetery gates,

I hear them making their cold calls,
reciting their breathless sales pitch
to the widows and beaten men.

Where I Would Cast My Last Lure

Somewhere bottomless
where no one will ever find its trembling
blue feathers, its pinched blue
wires, little false fireflies
of its eyes;

into the deepest river, water so cold
and dark, even the angels in all their radiance
would be obscured there;

where it could hide
weightless in Nothing's cobalt
ripples, the cyanine current
of void,

drifting down
     and
           down, and

    down

       like

   a word

fleshed in tassels
of bone.

Portrait of My Mother as a Japanese Paper Flower

I watch her drift
gradually

down

through the waters
of oblivion.

Her suffering-glass
is full.

Let me paint the world
in kimono colors
for her.

Let me arrange
a few spare words
like *ikebana*.

She is
tiny and dry.

Her weariness is gaudy
against the gray
December sky.

She beckons like a stuck
petal, one rehabbed arm
waving death closer:

Open
slowly,
Death.

Aphasia

She tries to express—
with a flutter, a wave of bony fingers
venous age-spotted skin—
                    a thought-flit
                    in camouflage

about trees in the sun
pink buds, cumulous clouds
of pollens, bees

—in flight toward
an idea-flower
—syllables—words

like *plum blossom*, the branches
fanned out above us

in the warm spring
light—words that dust her but fly
                    away, erratic, full
                    of their own sweet

powers
(or is the right
word "powders?")

She's cut loose from language
in a wounded brain cell cocoon.

My Mother at the Museum of Bound Feet

Golden Lotuses
like toddler booties—

"cranes for long life,"
silvered wings where

bones were broken:
toes, young child-soles

folded under. From her
wheelchair my mother

>   points to a dime-sized
>   peony embroidered

>   in gold: "*wizard stitchery...*"
—She can't speak;

half-blind since
her stroke, she's often

>   confused; the nerves
>   on her right side

dead but: born in 1919,
a year before suffrage,

outrage
can still spark.

>   Everything she has
>   left tingles with it.

The Parting

It was November outside—
the leaf-colored sofa inside
strangely vivid in the flickering

light,

as if someone had died
and lounged with new-found
brightness on the depressed
cushions.

Your heart
in its pink handkerchief
was hidden.

So I looked
down at your shoes
for some signal,

as if, in the moonlight,
they might be two rare
flowers blooming along
my way—but no,

they were only shoes,
unlacing themselves,
two tight wingtips
of shadow.

Sixty-Nine

1.

The rain is pouring down
the streetlights are lit

      the fishbone trees
wishbone branches
    are bowing and shivering

(snowing inside, ponds icing over
—waiting

     for the first incautious
                footstep)
Yesterday
I was sixty-eight

2.

The few leaves left
    on the poplars look
        like they are chatting
over a backyard
cloud-fence

      —or plotting
their unlikely escape

The street-
light bulbs have become bright
      eggs in a frosted glass
cage

3.

More pummel
and splash   gutter music
      downspout fugue

I am a marshland
              a swamp
(I have lived many years
in a floodplain)

4.

High winds tonight   great

        wild gusts

Old Cemetery Proofs

Eight darkening stills:
A litmus the acid years
are shadowing.

Emmanuel
Clothilde
Jonas

Wilhelmina
Ezekiel
Carmelita

Rachel
Jeremiah

Focused and refocused
in an underwater light
near the Sacramento

River, close enough to snap
the rippling olive fringe
of cottonwoods along the levee.

What had I hoped to capture
in each black and white frame
with my F stops and filters
in the city of old fashioned names?

As I adjusted my zoom lens
and scribbled my notes
a century after

the church bells fell silent
and the mourners turned home
in a pea soup tule,
wearing muddy boots,

or spit-shined high-buttons,
gliding past one another
like shades—

Feeding Tube

It isn't the pleated plastic
snake, or the mouth they cut
into her stomach to suck it—

it isn't the accordion of the lungs
squeezing out the laborious
hymns of exhalation

but the mobile of paper
birds her family hung *so hopefully*
over her bed—wild tropical birds,
macaws and toucans, parrots
and cockatoos—that I remember,

how the shadows of the birds
tethered to their wires drifted
over her like wild angels.

Visiting a Friend in Hospice

From where I sat beside her,
a rotating fan was positioned

on the floor out of sight
beyond the open kitchen door,

its low, continuous
whir...whir... whir... whir...

sounded like the solemn chant
of monks in processional

while the wall across from us
was suddenly lit with shadows

of leaves and vines in triangular frames
so they looked like stained glass windows

in a chapel built of reflection.
I sat quietly, watching and listening

while she slipped into a deep
slumber, her head bowed, her spine

slumped forward, chin resting
on her black embroidered blouse.

Her hands were clasped together
and the oxygen tube snaked

through the tangle of sheets;
the colorful flower stitchery

on her blouse rose and fell, rose
and fell in silence.

Cypress

The needles of the cypress
          outside hang between
me and a small slice
of clear blue

pie some call heaven—
          blueberries and milk,
the kingdom of the blessed
dead in a mixer

of starlight;
          the blades whir,
the beaters spin—*froth*
of resurrection?

Where did they go?
          Where have they been
transported to
on their gurneys

of air?

II.

Ansel Adams: Two Photographs

1.

"Graduation Dress"
    Yosemite Valley, 1948

She'd love to climb
the Jeffrey pine he's posed
her under—

find a toehold in scabs
of bark and shinny
up out of the girl

body unruffled (frills,
billows; skirt flared
like a bell—

Who'll ring her?)
Her underwear's simple
chemise—no bones but

a look that says
wire in her spine
when she's grown.

2.

"Woman Behind Screen Door "
            Independence, CA, 1944

Her look says
life's for the birds

(it's mostly her mouth
that says so)

while little white hearts
cascade down the front
of her dress

or are they stars
in the night sky,
the entire

Milky Way spilt
down her indigo
jersey? No,

they're hearts
after all.

There's the whine
of mosquitoes, flutter
of white moths—

they're drawn
to her but can't
get in—

*So this
is Independence...*

knuckle flesh
swollen around her
wedding ring.

It might as well be
the veil of truth
she's posed behind.

Adam and Eve at Seventy

After Man and Woman, *a sculpture by Linda Gelfman*

The woman is all
deflated breasts, wasted

hips; his collapsed
belly hunkers

over a puny sex.
(He could be

crunching a Havana
from the crimp

of his lips.
She tastes

something tiny,
a thimble

of poison.)
Shrunken apple

doll faces...
Why can't they

just fuse into self
knowledge?

Their lumped skulls
look bashed,

as if a mutual
dream had been

punched.

O'Keeffe's *Pedernal*

Where are the people on the Pedernal?
    The dusky sloping bodies
        of women and their dislocated
           men—scattered like lost

bones in the permanent summer twilight.
    Are they standing stone still
        in the pulsing, lung-colored hills—
           rooted like light-washed stumps

out of our view, or are they turning
    to look back at us, like Lot's wife,
        their bewildered footprints
          tangled in piñon

needles, mineral flecks, schist?
    Oh they are foolhardy
        if they have let themselves
          be led up there
         alone.

Carousel Quilt

A stallion snorts scraps
of lilac pongee.

The sun is an orchid
idea, thinly snipped

to twelve cymbidium
rays—a hothouse sun.

Swamps, fingerlakes,
savannah shapes

are joined to recreate
an equine anatomy—

cushy fetlocks, withers,
locked in a puffy levade;

a tendon patched from
an old flannel sleeper,

batted fat to a flank.
Nosegays, leaves in forest

greens, roses for the carousel's
wide canopy, so

the dreaming mind rides
under a hood of woods

and fragrance, ferns and musk,
so the wildness inside us

rears its head, and our eyes
roll upward to heaven—chintz

pie wedges pieced under
French knot clouds.

Imagining the Woman in Hopper's *Automat*

He has stilled the nerves
in her thick cup, the rattle
of the chipped

saucer, the shaky
clink clink clink,
like porcelain chimes—

even the ripple of thought
in her forehead has slowed,
become a fixed
white clock.

Her thoughts can wind
down in this space.

A slowed pulse beats
under one gloved thumb.

Only herself to think about now...

The infinite night outside is a black
scriptorium, a blank jet screen.

Raphael's *Woman with Unicorn*

Her necklace, knotted
gold filigree with its chunk
of polished lapidary

(cochineal ruby with pear
shaped pearl drop), hangs
like suspense over her

breast—like a stopped
clock's pendulum.
Her arms form a perfect

basketry around the puppy-
sized *liocorno* tucked up
against her womb.

Its spike looks small
but dangerous.

Gift Quilt Square with Artichokes and Stars

for my daughter

Pinch the bud of looking
back: You'll see

she's hardy. All her honey sticks
to the bee balm and hyssop colors,
to the cuttings of deep green

like basil and woodruff
with a ground cover
of thick white stars.

I think that her fingers on the needles
were orderly and anise-scented
like sweet fennel. And look

how she has softened
even the artichoke's central
theme, pushed two repeating
rows of barbed petals to the fringes
where they can't help
blossoming like big peonies
on black slabs of cheap duck.

The center square is solo
choke—the tough lotus
unfolding, its head chopped off
so we stare into its silkiest
well, a sage moon
smudged with eclipse.

It is my gift to look at
and touch her trellis of tints;
to imagine her path through the woods
as even handstitch
sown like mail order seed
tapes along the windblown borders
of dollhouse linoleum checks
in shadow and lime, binding
the whole together, fencing it
in anticipation of wind, the unleafing
edges—turning under what frays.

Diane Arbus: *Two Ladies at the Automat*

They pose with the sugar
jar, a sweetness
like the cane's

white death.
> *Les Demoiselles*
D'Automat.

The one with the fake
Russian hat scrunched
over her pageboy points

a pearly fingernail
to hell, or else

she is tapping
a filed-down message
in personal Morse

(like inmates rap)
through smears of Cremora:

Dear Mama:
Look how our lives keep
going on without you.

Rembrandt's Late Self-Portraits

Their lit-from-within moons god
only knows what terrors—

that polished scorch
mark gloom, that burned-up
letters of hope char

in the lustrous dim.
They shine like Cro-Magnon
skulls out of the frontal
past. They pulse with

the energy of the soul's
primal blast.

The Artist as a God of Winter

after Milton Avery's Road to the Sea

It's silent over those blue trees   scratched in
                              like cold seeds
onto the white slopes.

                              The half-gelled
ocean is sluggish, subdued,   where the artist dragged
                              his knife to scrawl

          in the midnight tides.
Who could survive

such cold? In the distance, glacial
                              peaks block any other
          vista. Storm gathers

the long white ledge of a distant
                              hill. Not one
blue curl of smoke rises

                    to warm
the icy souls huddled
                    beneath his frozen
rooftops.

          Is this the arctic road
we all must travel
          to reach home?

Landscape After Charles Burchfield

Rows of houses crisscross the horizon
        on the other side of a cyclone
                fence; they shimmer, looking

alive and haunted, as flocks of field
        sparrows sweep the margins between
                earth and sky, song and silence,

and a crow holds court on a gleaming aerial,
        solo: *Poets are the antennae of the race,*
                he announces, having memorized Pound.

There is a pond nearby, and sometimes
        it turns to ice, unable to bear any human
                weight; but it's spring today,

the grasses blazing coolly electric, sun
        in a clotted corona of clouds.

H is for Heron

Black-Crowned Night Heron, blue moon like an eye
looking out at us from blue sky. Life raft moon—

or the sun in blue eclipse? Target moon? Heron won't ask,
won't answer why an open window of sea hangs beside him—

chalkboard sea, opalescent shell (or is it a sail?) shining;
two more eyes, or beads, or blue inner tubes adrift on blue

waves scratched in. Two twigs, four leaves, ghost-twigs,
ghost-leaves. Two blue streaks, electric, like blue thoughts:

A road, an undulant path marked in blue, making a blue
music like Picasso's *Blue Guitar*—or two snipped strands (Clotho's

threads?) afloat in the fleeting world; two lifelines
leading to Heron, its alert hypnotic hunter's eye, its look of mild

consternation: *What shall I do now? Where shall I go
next? How shall I fish the deep waters called Home?*

Bruegel: *Landscape with the Fall of Icarus*

It's my heart, antic bird—flying with wax
        paper wings—too close to the sun's
            skullcap of fire. Little black

        tar shack.
               Little singed
        tongue,

        still
singing—

III.

Audio

I am listening to the maple tree, the finches
in the hedge beneath and around it, that rhythmic

flutter of yellow feathers and the gusts of maple
breath from the jittery winged seeds.

I'm thinking of how quickly the soil will be littered
with its bright, fallen leaves, the amber-reds

drying into crunchable maps, farewell letters
from the country of autumn—the finches

long gone—the past, this moment, a ghostly
replay in imagination's ear.

"Costs of War Mount for Russia, and for Civilians in Ukraine"

New York Times, March 9, 2022

Temperature slightly above freezing,
chill winds inside.

My eyelids flutter and twitch
above the headlines,

the nerves in my hands tremble
and tingle.

Outside the flowering pears
have dropped all their petals—

they blanket the sidewalks and yards
like fallen snow. Today's news

takes root, the cracks in the planet
icing us down, exposed.

Yesterday periwinkles, dandelions,
oxalis, crow—

I prayed to them all as I walked past
the neighborhood's showcase of wild

survival, the altars of beauty
and soon-to-be

ruin. The redbuds are exploding
into harmless flame.

Eclipse

total eclipse but

for a while it wears a thin
white skullcap, a widow in mourning
in a Far Eastern country of endless
star-time and space—

an ancient widow mourning across the clear night sky
banging the gong, the drum we recognize
as bloodrush, the whir and thump
of our temporary hearts.

Driving home I see my elderly
neighbors, the two of them out on their lawn,
leaning into each other, skinny
as dime-store telescopes.

Maybe the moon is grieving for them, wailing
and crying in advance of the day
they will exit alone

into the houses of ash and bone.

Tightrope Sonnet

Darkness in the light,
lightness in the dark,
each star a shining leaf,
a leaf full of star fragrance.

The creatures of night
swallow it down,
the mockingbird in hiding
gulps it in. Soon a woman

starts to write a song
then loses it. Silence showers,
erasures spark. No words,
no praises, only daylight now,

the frankness of mockingbird
on his favorite high wire.

Fire Season

Driving home from the ocean,
from foam coils like lacy sand dollars
pasted to shore, fog banks boogie boarding
in with the evening surfers, we see

smoke clouds, sooty sky-islands,
wildfire tides rolling toward us.
I think of caddis flies, midges, leaf-
hoppers, snout moths, click beetles—

swallowtails and mourning cloaks,
wolf spiders, orb-weavers, silk slingers,
all those non-human universes
exploding into flame—how

we breathe them in, how they drift
into our lungs on wisps of char-vapor
while firefighters try to hold the line
and evacuated humans wait

in uncertainty's wings. These days
our hearts feel like umbels of drought-
stressed sweet fennel, dry spikelets
of quaking grass or brome.

Reading a Ghost's Book of Poems

I woke this morning with two bright blood dots
in my palms—tiny blood roses
between the heart and life

lines. The ghost's book was on the table
beside me. The poems knew she is
a ghost. They understood

she is one of the disappeared though her pulse
thumps on inside them, though they wear
her bones, her sorrows, exhale

the world through her lungs; though her words
still rush along inside their veins
like blood.

Turbulence

Flying in from Denver we hit
        turbulence, and dropped

three thousand feet all at once.

I thought
        the dry gold hills are rising
                to meet us...

but the wings
leveled and the plane

        surged forward toward

equilibrium—the direction
        fear takes when we give it up
                to the buffeting winds.

We landed safely.
It was raining

        to re-remind us how we are strung
                to the shiftless heavens.

I thought:
        I'm home again... and stood in odd
                lavender-colored light

        waiting for you.
I let the wet silt over me—

I let it comment
    on all I'd been thinking.

I let the big drops splash
    my gray sweater
        with dark stars.

Flashback

The wild geese take flight
low along the railroad tracks...

My poet-friend sends me a Masaoka Shiki
postcard from Oakland. I hold my pen

like a single lonely chopstick and write back
on a Georgia O'Keeffe.

Once I poured rice wine liberally
over fresh-steamed rice, fanned it

with a Hiroshige fan, smoothed out
sheets of Nori to make sushi

from scratch— the method my Japanese
exchange student roommate taught me

before she eloped one night with a born-again
biker from Missoula;

before the pink dial phone rang, her parents
at the other end, in Toyko:

Who? Where? When?
I never heard from her again.

It was the Sixties. The rent was due,
The phone bill arrived on schedule.

Photograph of Your Father Sewing Needlepoint at Precinct Headquarters, 1956

His athletic body tilted back,
his big tired "dogs"
in their polished wing-tips

propped up on the cluttered
desk. At ease—
stocky index and thumb

tugging the yarn taut, as though it was
the most natural thing
in the world for a burly

detective, a tough Irish cop
in 1950's New York,
to design and sew needlepoint

cushions for the parlor chairs
when only hours before,
as the department's crime

scene photographer, he'd snapped
the cold postures brutality
crafts—all the horrors

he hoped with every fiber
of his being you
would never see.

The Letter

Ten o'clock: weak sunlight. A hand pauses
halfway down the page. A letter in the mind,
a few round syllables unwritten.

As when a shadow walks out into a fallow field
where snow has fallen, covering the blanks
where roses might have grown;

or when a traveler dreams her way into another
country, to find the map of a man there,
her confused lover.

The letter will never be signed and sent
in this life. A thumb presses down on an invisible
thorn of presence, and blood beads up.

The Bumblebee

It looks
clumsy and widowish
      gathering its bucket
            of fruits. A glassy black
            jewel

in the ring of the Bishop
      of Danger. "I feel like
            I'm living on the edge
            of a cliff,"

      says a friend,
whose lover has Alzheimer's.
      The bee licks
            a lilac's vapors, lips
            the pollen's shellac,

self-absorbed.
      It works itself free
            like a glossy knot
            in the slippery blue

      rope
of morning, then vanishes again
      to some cool hive
            in the eaves.
      When it's gone

I cut and arrange
      the bee's damp vessels
            in the quiet sacristy
            of leaves.

Lament for the Flowering Pear Tree In Our Back Yard

It resembles
                    a crucifixion—now that the men
        in their helmets, their bucket-trucks
have come
                    and gone, and the severed limbs
                            have fallen, and the leaves
        have been cleared,
and the few remaining

branches sag
            into the humid
dusk.

What is done cannot be
                undone, the inner priest
        pronounces.

                        We paid. It was necessary

to save what might be lost
                        in a sudden breaking
            away,

                to guard the passers by
        who sheltered briefly
in its shade.

Soon the stars will come out to grieve
                                and spangle
the cold night
sky above the tree's fresh
wounds. *Cleave,*

Cleave...

Enlightenment

I did not know the red
currants in the earthenware bowl
were a symbol of Christ's
final sacrifice, or that

strawberries are the food
of the blessed and therefore evoke
the image of Earthly Paradise,
as it says here in my book,

*The Symbols of Nature
and Art*, spread open on a yellow
table in the Pine Cone Diner
at Point Reyes Station,

where I am listening to a glad-
iolus' red chat and music—
observing its swoop of trumpet
swan neck shake loose

a few scarlet feathers against
an orange chair—

Evening Song At Stinson Beach

the faraway brimming   the weather altered

the clouds were dwindling
     a heron dived   a mussel clung

the sea whispered its cold   mysteries
—of salt chapels   brine parables

we were lulled by the melody
the soul-moan   the melancholy

tone-rivers   syncopated
chords that seemed so   human:

Weary   piano   of the heart
play on—

Elegy for a Beloved Poet

We gathered together in the night—
you with your tiger-eye; the night was
poetry. Your poems were skyscrapers—
the moon and stars shone down on them—
there was also a galaxy inside each window.
We stared up at the staggering grandeur,
a city at night, built of your words.
Some of us were dressed for the cold countries,
others had palm trees inside their hearts
but all of us were wearing the many-colored cloaks
of astonishment. Where are you now, poet
of the oceans, poet of the air,
poet whose words climbed the highest
mountains, dove into the deepest wells—
I will hold them to my heart. I will live
in your city of words until the breath
is stolen from me.

>Gathered in the night
>we saw the light inside you.

for Dennis Schmitz, 1937-2019

Angina

However early it will be
the denial of light, the arrival of dawn,
you breathe, you sleep, and the moon rises
like a shiver of silvered light—dreams are
forgotten, waves that splashed, friends
that died, ladders you climbed until
your thumping heartbeat wakes you
and you chew the aspirin, let it dissolve
like yesterdays under your tongue.

IV.

Estate Sale

The white kitchen table stood
outside on the lawn beside blue
liriope and a dark four poster.

Three spindle back chairs sat
off in one corner as strangers
pulled to the curb, talking price.

The day grew hot; the yard
held the heat until the late shade
gathered it. Deep in shadow

the ghosts convened, polite
guests returning to the scene,
too courteous to make a fuss.

The Moon Bee

The moon bee is made
of frost. She wanders

the halls of underleaves
at midnight

and sucks the shine
from silvered pistils.

Her sting is quick,
a frozen

bite—iced
venom, if you cross her

path like chance.
Tonight

she hums
in a groove of shadow,

solo.
She breathes

the groves
of deep song in.

After the War

Honolulu, T.H.

We collected bullets and bees
We trapped them in jars
And when a bee stung me
I thought it was a bullet
Hidden in a lehua blossom
I was wounded
We were all wounded
In my grandmother's garden
In the bungalow's side yard
With its thick rind of mud
And leftover war
With the lehuas's soft red spines
That's why we pretended to be wild
Horses galloping, mares whinnying
Stallions rearing and snorting
That's why we coughed up Kool-aid blood
We wanted to fool the neighbors
We wanted to show them what
Wounded meant to Portuguese
Immigrants, to the grandchildren
Of Portuguese immigrants
With hammers and nails we punctured
The jars' lids, ready to trap bees
Which were really bullets after all
We made air holes
So the bullets could breathe
Many years later they tethered
My grandmother to a chair on the Mainland

It was after the Poor House
It was before Medicare
They roped her up and tied her in
(She had tried to run out the door to Hawaii)
It was snowing
The streets were strange and full of traffic
The cupboards were lined with jam jars
Strawberry, raspberry, apricot and grape
And on the shelves between them
Many dead bees
It was the bees, my grandmother insisted
Who had given their lives
For their country

Teaching Poetry in the Prisons

I think of him
as a victim
(a veteran)

of war—
every day was
the enemy

in a house-
hold that thought

children should
be punished
with barbed wire,

belts, burns, punches,
pinches, slaps, kicks,

starvation. Where meth
was the vitamin,
sex was the money,

where poverty was
the neighborhood,

poverty was
the country

and nobody ever
called him honey

until high school
freed him to be

part of something
larger than himself,

a gang. They robbed
a convenience
store; someone got

shot, killed—he did not
pull the trigger yet

here he is twenty
years later, life

without parole—
shaking my hand,
smiling at me,

thanking me
for helping him learn

one new word.

Tutoring Center

Yuba City, CA 1964

Where a friend and I once taught at the Richland Housing Center,
the rows of Quonsets on treeless lanes have been replaced
by K-Marts and tracts.

The heat is the same—I remember stewing in it
with a do-gooder's shock at the mattress for six
on the bare dirt floor,

the unplugged icebox, the four kids chattering excitedly to us
in Spanish, all at once. (Their mother offered rellenos
and we ate.)

We prepared to teach, named two made-over corrugated shacks
"Library" and "School," with signs we scratched on poster
board with black markers.

We brought books, paper, pens, with the help of Mr. Alvarez from County
Welfare, and we began (though some kids—even the youngest—
vamoosed to earn and pick). Summer passed.

Some college volunteers from Berkeley came, took over, and we
became high school students again. That was also the year
of drunkenness and despair—

my father overdosed on whiskey and pills, and I turned to the Church.
Mass was in Spanish each Sunday evening and I was lifted
by the choir's labors—

braceros whose ripe voices toiled
to spill their gold
for free.

Aftershock

Two houses down a family has moved out, U-Haul
        vanished, father headed for prison, For Sale
              sign up on the lawn. Where

will his three children be ten, twenty, thirty
        years from now? What will they remember?
              Later today when I sit in a cellblock

with the men from A Yard, they'll write poems that show
        how memory can burst so unexpectedly
              into flower, and I'll see my own sad father

again, an apparition being led away in handcuffs, chains.
        Extradition. My eighth winter.

Recurring Nightmare

The same old darkness wakes you:
the white glove raises the curtain, the bald puppeteer
jerks every nerve, snaps every string.

> *A man who calls himself Daddy,*
> *a stranger you have never*
> *seen, leans over your white crib—*

> > *the whiskey*
> > *breath, the slurred*
> > *cooing—*

> *You are too young to be terrified*
> *but your heart remembers*
> *to pretend*

> *it is a small pink rattle when*
> *he picks you up and shakes you.*

You throw off the quilt
with its myth of lilies and roses, its fairy tale
of warmth and even stitches.

How will you travel the next lightless hour,
trailing the torn hem of sleep, to the kitchen,
the bright window of morning—
the pots of fuchsias filling with sunlight,
the tea kettle, singing its one song,
its one homely hymn?

You want only to release the morning
like its own white dove, want it to return to you
with its sprig of olive.

Summer Solstice

Morning heats up
like a topaz jewel.
By noon the matchstick

grasses look like beaten
gold if you squint
against the June sheen.

Once you touched the burning
plexus, the naked fiery hive
of tormented passion alive

inside the body of another
summer, and lived.

Assemblage

The past rearranges itself before me:
A bride and groom like paper dolls

snipped from old postcards—*pastiche?*
collage? She is made of a day-tripper's

imaginary *Wanderjahr* in Paris, an afternoon
at the Louvre—the groom is all Iowa, wind

in the cornfields. Above them the full moon,
(*l'amour...*) like an exotic but familiar

postage stamp the color of an ancient
coin. Something in the sky snaps shut,

the future's cold black purse. (Inside
her heart is a firefly: luminosity, then

flight!)

Passing By

I was thinking how we all suffer
eventually, a kind of accidental
spiritual whiplash—

a death, a bad marriage,
debts—when I saw the old
couple waiting for the bus;

sitting on the brick edge
of an empty planter box,
the earth in it torn up,

as if someone in a rage
had pulled the flowers up
by their throats.

The woman stared off
into space absently,
as if thinking of some life

she'd lost. Her face
was heavily powdered,
a chalky scrim

for two poppy rouge
spots on her cheeks.
Her neck was in a brace;

her skull dotted its latex "i"
like a bud on a palsied stem.
The old man was turned

toward her in a half-twist,
like a landlocked diver—
his entire attention focused

on her, the only fine fish
in his sea—or, as if she was
the last magic flower,

the single most fragrant
and holy petal at the center
of his universe.

The two of them looked so
vulnerable there, as the bus pulled up
and they climbed in,

smoky leaves of exhaust
curling around them.

Elegy

To dust go the earrings and bracelets.
To smoke go the glamorous wrists.
Each noble earlobe, each Egyptian eye,

to smoke; to dust.
To dust go the motes, the specks of truth.
To dust go the earrings and bracelets.

To dust go the toenails, the shyness, the ruse
of hope; the silver curls, the high cheekbones.
Each noble earlobe, each Egyptian eye,

to erasure, to oblivion. To never go
the heartbeats, the miseries.
To dust go the earrings and bracelets.

To fire and smoke. To dust
go the compulsions, the aphasia, the obsessions.
Each noble earlobe, each Egyptian eye.

To dust, each eyelash. To flame,
the pelvic bones, the femurs, the ribs.
To dust go the earrings and bracelets.
Each noble earlobe, each Egyptian eye.

> To dust.

August

I wish I believed
the soul could rise
from its matted nest
of hair and bone,
its messy web
of flesh tints gloomy

blood hymns—
squeezing up and out
through the skull's trap
door, into the invisible
night of eternal
mystery—

rocketing like mercury
toward the secret
attic where god
keeps all the dead
cool and terminal
with mercy

but I'm stuck
at a window above
the scorched spathes
of arum lilies, watching
my father's tired ghost
haunt the garden.

A saguaro stands
beside him like the spiny
pitiless hand of a god;
the only angel out there
is sad, half-chewed, lit
by the Dog Star.

Old Family Goblet

Vaguely I see the world rainbowed in it,
a reflection like Tarot's upside down cups—
the elements of the past made transparent;
future's inherited look. Sometimes the cut-glass
face of betrayal shows up in it, as when one lives with
a perfect thing long enough to chip its shining
rim.(Think of all the lips it has touched!)
It can be hard to hold onto
a clear idea of
fragility—
the mind
is such a
slippery
place,
with such
sharp edges.
Always the waters of sadness abide there.

Our Hope

wears an evening gown
has feathers like a dove
closes the casket lid
over the bones of disaster

lights the lantern
switches on the light
has the beloved child's
radiant face

our hope
is a long letter written in cursive
an origami crane
a fresh sweet wind

it flutters toward us
out of the center
of the storm, perches
on a skyscraper, a billboard
a church spire—

it is both airborne and land borne
it tumbles along in the rapids
over rock, it drifts like a leaf
in the slowest currents

it has no shape
but it is a cloud of knowing
woven like the warmest sweater
on the coldest day
out of simple amazement

Confluence

A mile from here two rivers meet,
two strangers talking river-talk,
befriending each other,
joining hands for the long trip home.

Those of us who live beside them
watch their water levels rise and fall.
In our dreams we hear them breathing
and the currents become exhalations.

Tonight we'll stand along the pebbled shore
like herons and egrets, necks craned
skyward, as the wolf moon disappears
into total eclipse, blood moon.

Rain will fall, storms will blow in
but we will stand there, planted
among the cattails and willows.

We will think we are still dreaming
when the ghosts of the mothers and fathers arrive,
when they hold hands with us, singing.

Plainsong

There is so much of ruin in the world's sick
        tumult, but spring arrives anyway.

A hummingbird zeroes in on a barely open abutilon
        blossom (fierce traveler!)

while the dogwood stands at attention—a graceful
        pink-capped sentinel—

and the April wind plays its peaceful violins. Deep
        in the earth-veins, the spirit-monks are singing

their own Gregorian chants. The rest of us hide
        our gloomy hearts, as the skies rain down

all this potable light.

Psalm for Sunrise

Let starlight fade in the East.

Let the horses of dreaming ramble
home slowly from their sweet dark pastures.

Let the sun nourish us like wheat.

Let me tidy the quilts
and the flesh-scented sheets.

Let my feet step forth gently
and my heart pump strongly.

Let the kettle cry out
on its bed of blue flame.

Let bee song and crow song rise.

Let the sound of the waking city arise
and the day in its glory bless us.

Notes

Most of the poems collected here were published in magazines and anthologies from the 1980s through 2023. A smaller number of the poems appear here for the first time.

Section II is composed entirely of ekphrastic poems, including:

> "Adam and Eve at Seventy" after *Man and Woman*, a sculpture by Linda Gelfman.

> "H is for Heron" for Frankie Hansbearry, after her ceramic painting, *Black-Crowned Night Heron*.

Additional dedications:

> "Visiting a Friend on Hospice" is for Jane, in memory.

> "Reading a Ghost's Book of Poems" is for C.D. Wright, in memory.

> "Flashback" is for Judy H.

> "Photograph of Your Father Sewing Needlepoint at Precinct Headquarters, 1956" is for David, John and Chris

> "Elegy for a Beloved Poet" is for Dennis Schmitz, 1937-2019

Acknowledgments

Many thanks to the editors and journals where the following poems first appeared, sometimes in earlier versions::

Aesthetica: "Cold Call"
Alimentum: "Last Supper"
Anacapa Review: "Summer Solstice"
Caliiope: "Aphasia"
Canary: "Lament for the Flowering Pear Tree in our Backyard"
Carquinez Review: "August"
Cloudbank: "Frangible Operas"
Comstock Review: "Portrait of my Mother as a Japanese Paper Flower"
   (Muriel Craft Bailey Poetry Prize finalist)
Cortland Review: "The Parting" and "Sixty-Nine"
Cosumnes River Journal: "Old Cemetery Proofs"
Dogwood: "Songs for the End of Spiritual Winter"
Ekphrasis: "Ansel Adams: Woman Behind Screen Door," "Ansel Adams:
   Graduation Dress," "Breugel: The Fall of Icarus," "Carousel Quilt,"
   and "Raphael's Woman with Unicorn"
Evening Street Review: "Evening Song at Stinson Beach"
Heliotrope: "Turbulence"
Hospital Drive: "Feeding Tube"(poetry prize finalist)
International Literary Quarterly: "Rembrandt's Late Self-Portraits"
Levure Litteraire: "The Letter"
MacGuffin: "Plainsong" and "The Bumblebee"
Montserrat Review: "Gift Quilt Square with Artichoke and Stars,"
   "O'Keeffe's Pedernal"
Mudlark: "Visiting a Friend in Hospice," "Cypress," "Landscape After
   Charles Birchfield," "H is for Heron," "Audio," "Costs of War Mount
   for Russia and for Civilians in Ukraine," "Eclipse," and "Tightrope
   Sonnet"
Passages North: "Two Ladies at the Automat"
Poet Lore: "Estate Sale"
Poetry Flash: "Elegy for a Beloved Poet"

PoetryMagazine.com: "Reading a Ghost's Book of Poems," "Flashback"
Postcard Poems: "Enlightenment"
Prairie Schooner: "Angina"
Red Wheelbarrow: "After the War" (poetry prize finalist)
Rosebud: "Where I Would Cast my Last Lure"(William Stafford Poetry
    Prize finalist)
Smartish Pace: "Late Alzheimer's" (Erskine J Poetry Prize, finalist)
The High Window: "Passing By," "Our Hope," "Confluence"
Vox Populi: "Photograph of Your Father Sewing Needlepoint at Precinct
    Headquarters, 1956"
Weber: The Contemporary West: "Parallel Worlds"
Writers Resist: "Teaching Poetry in the Prisons"

Thanks also to the editors of the anthologies below for including these
poems:
    "Magnificat," *Fog and Woodsmoke* (Lost Hills Press, 2011)
    "Korea, 1952," *The Hermit Kingdom, Poems of the Korean War* (Center
        for the Study of the Korean War, 1995)
    "My Mother at the Museum of Bound Feet," *Veils, Haloes and Shackles,*
        International Poetry on the Oppression and Empowerment of Women
        (Kasva Press, 2016)
    "Fire Season," *California Fire and Water* (Story Street Press, 2020)
    "Tutoring Center," "Aftershock," "Recurring Nightmare," "Assemblage,"
        "Psalm for Sunrise," and "Confluence," *Voices Anthology* (Cold River
        Press, 2023)
    "The Moon Bee," *Know Me Here* (Word Temple Press, 2017)

Deep bow and many thanks to David Starkey and Chryss Yost of Gunpowder
Press for their continued support and generosity. It has, once again, been such
an honor and privilege to work with them.

I also want to express my ongoing gratitude to the poets, editors and dear
friends whose support, advice, encouragement, and friendship have sustained
me over the years--especially Sandra McPherson, Joshua McKinney, William
Slaughter, Joyce Jenkins, Mary Mackey, Ilya Kaminsky, Russell Thorburn,
Hannah Stein, Shawn Pittard, Mary Moore, and poetry pals, Mary Zeppa,

Kathleen Lynch, Lisa Dominguez Abraham, Victoria Dalkey, Catherine French, our dear Carol Frith, who passed away in 2020, and my beloved mentor Dennis Schmitz, who passed away in 2019.

Big thanks also to William O'Daly, Susan Cohen, Dean Rader and Joyce Jenkins for their inspiring words about this book. And, finally, biggest thanks as always to my partner in life, David DeWitt, and to my children, Jennifer and Michael, and my son-in-law Michael Shen for being the delightful and creative people they are.

ABOUT THE POET

Sacramento resident Susan Kelly-DeWitt is a former Wallace Stegner Fellow. Her previous collection, *Gatherer's Alphabet,* was published by Gunpowder Press in 2022 as the inaugural book in the California Poets Series. She is also the author of *Gravitational Tug* (Main Street Rag Publishing, 2020), *Spider Season* (Cold River Press, 2016), *The Fortunate Islands* (Marick Press, 2008), and a number of previous small press and online collections. Her work has also appeared in many anthologies, and in print and online journals at home and abroad, recently as the featured American Poet in the UK journal *The High Window*. Her past professional and writing life includes having been a reviewer for *Library Journal*, the editor-in-chief of the online journal *Perihelion*, the Program Director of the Sacramento Poetry Center and the Women's Wisdom Arts Program, a Poet in the Schools and a Poet in the Prisons, a blogger for *Coal Hill Review*, and a longtime instructor for the UC Davis Division of Continuing Education. She is currently a member of the National Book Critics Circle, the Northern California Book Reviewers Association and a contributing editor for *Poetry Flash*. She is also an exhibiting visual artist. Please visit her website at www.susankelly-dewitt.com.

ALSO FROM
GUNPOWDER PRESS

www.ingramcontent.com/pod-product-compliance
Lightning Source LLC
Chambersburg PA
CBHW031440120626
46545CB00006B/2497